William Pitt Mason

Notes on Qualitative Analysis

Arranged for Students Use

William Pitt Mason

Notes on Qualitative Analysis
Arranged for Students Use

ISBN/EAN: 9783744666701

Printed in Europe, USA, Canada, Australia, Japan

Cover: Foto ©Paul-Georg Meister /pixelio.de

More available books at **www.hansebooks.com**

NOTES

—ON—

QUALITATIVE ANALYSIS,

ARRANGED FOR THE USE OF STUDENTS

OF THE

Rensselaer Polytechnic Institute,

—BY—

W. P. MASON,

Professor of Chemistry.

THIRD EDITION.

EASTON, PA.:
CHEMICAL PUBLISHING CO.
1896.

PREFACE.

THE market is unquestionably much overstocked with books upon this subject, and the author's only excuse for making this addition to the number is that it meets the requirements of his own classes.

There is small doubt that, were it not for the expense of printing, every teacher of chemistry would use a text-book made by himself with either pen or scissors, for the sufficient reason that it is more acceptable to both the instructor and the student to use a book from cover to cover, rather than to cut and omit material from a work more voluminous than the class requires.

The attempt has been made in these notes to induce the student to make use of works of reference. It is to be regretted that the energies are often bent towards blindly following the words of the text without ever attempting to "read between the lines;" but it is hoped that those who use what is here given may be led so to think for themselves as to create a desire to know rather than an anxiety to pass. Equations should be written under all the paragraphs, and the references should be examined in a most thorough manner. It is the author's practice to hold a daily "quiz-class" upon points of difficulty connected with the laboratory work; and he finds the results most satisfactory when a student is placed in charge of such a class and is required to answer such questions as may be asked by his fellow students.

The paragraphs in large print cover reactions upon

which the analytical tables are afterwards based, while those in smaller type often refer to technical rather than to analytical chemistry.

The scheme for the analysis of phosphates has been purposely omitted, in order that the beginner may not encounter too great difficulties at the start. Whenever, therefore, a phosphate is detected by the tests on page 33, and also a precipitate is obtained in the Iron Group, recourse must be had to more complete notes on Qualitative Analysis. If, however, no precipitate be found on testing for the Iron Group, the presence of a phosphate will not interfere with the use of the present tables.

RENSSELAER POLYTECHNIC INSTITUTE,
OCTOBER, 1896.

Reactions for the Basic Residues.

(The terms basic and acid residues are to be understood as follows : Suppose the base KOH to be acted upon by the acid H_2SO_4, the equation would be,

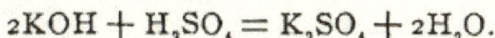

$$2KOH + H_2SO_4 = K_2SO_4 + 2H_2O.$$

The salt formed by this reaction consists of two distinct parts, or residues, *viz :* K_2 and SO_4. The former is derived from the original base, and is termed in consequence the basic residue ; the latter from the original acid, and is distinguished as the acid residue.)

Ammonium.—Use NH_4Cl.

1. Solid ammonium compounds, heated on platinum foil (not to bright redness), are completely volatilized.

2. KOH solution poured into a test-tube containing an ammonium compound in any form, and heated, gives off NH_3,—recognized by its smell and by its turning moistened red litmus paper blue. (The litmus paper should not be permitted to touch the liquid in the tube.)

3. $PtCl_4$ solution, added to a solution of NH_4Cl on a watch-glass, and stirred, gives a yellow crystalline precipitate of $(NH_4)_2PtCl_6$, which is soluble both in water and KOH, but insoluble in acids and alcohol.

4. Rub together, in a mortar, some dry NH_4Cl and dry lime. Note the smell. Is any gas evolved having a reaction on moistened litmus paper? Do solids ever react upon one another?—(*J. Soc. Chem. Ind.*, **7,** 567.)

5. Hold a rod moistened with strong HCl, near a dish containing a little NH$_4$OH. · Note and explain the result.

6. Place a mixture of dry NH$_4$Cl and dry BaSO$_4$ in a dry test-tube. Heat nearly to redness over a Bunsen burner. Cut the tube in two, and examine both residue and sublimate for "ammonium."

Was the separation of the two salts complete?

Potassium.—Use KCl.

7. When heated on platinum foil, potassium compounds do not volatilize at a low red heat (different from ammonium).

8. PtCl$_4$, added to a solution of KCl, which has been slightly acidified with HCl, gives a yellow precipitate of K$_2$PtCl$_6$. (In appearance this precipitate is not to be distinguished from the one produced in paragraph 3.)

9. *Flame Coloration.*—Potassium compounds, either solid or liquid, impart a *violet* color to the non-luminous Bunsen flame.

(In order to apply this and all other flame tests, make a small loop on the end of a platinum wire; dip this into the liquid under examination, and hold the adhering drop in the Bunsen flame. If the substance be a solid, moisten it with HCl before placing it in the flame.)

10. Burn some pieces of wood to an ash, moisten the ash with strong HCl and examine by spectroscope.—(*Watts' Dict.*, 4, 692.)

Sodium.—Use NaCl.

11. *Flame Coloration*—Yellow.

(This is a most delicate and reliable test, but where much sodium is present, the intensity of the color will mask the presence of other flame-giving metals. For list of flame colors see appendix.)

12. Burn some hard soap shavings to an ash, moisten with HCl, and take fláme and spectroscope reaction.

Magnesium.—Use solution of $MgSO_4$.

13. NH_4OH: white precipitate, $Mg(OH)_2$, easily soluble in NH_4Cl.

14. Na_2HPO_4 added after NH_4Cl and NH_4OH, gives a white precipitate of $MgNH_4PO_4$, which is readily soluble in acids.

(It is necessary to have an excess of NH_4OH in this case in order to render the $MgNH_4PO_4$ insoluble; and the presence of NH_4Cl is required to prevent the NH_4OH throwing down a white precipitate of $Mg(OH)_2$. See paragraph 13.

15. Some magnesium compounds, particularly the silicates, have a "soapy" feeling when rubbed between the fingers. Note also the lightness of such compounds as MgO and $MgCO_3$. What is Meerschaum?

16. Ignited before the blowpipe, magnesium compounds glow with a white light; and if the ignited mass be moistened with a solution of cobalt nitrate, and again ignited, it will assume a pink tint.

Calcium.—Use $CaCl_2$.

17. H_2SO_4: white precipitate of $CaSO_4$ forms imme-

diately in strong solutions. In weak solutions, boiling and long standing are necessary.

18. $(NH_4)_2CO_3$: white precipitate of $CaCO_3$, soluble in acetic acid.

19. K_2CrO_4: no precipitate. (Different from Ba and Sr, paragraphs 34 and 40.)

20. $(NH_4)_2C_2O_4$: white precipitate of CaC_2O_4, soluble in mineral acids; very insoluble in NH_4OH.

21. *Flame Coloration*—Red.

(Not readily distinguished from the strontium flame color without the aid of the spectroscope.)

22. Heat $CaCO_3$, Na_2CO_3 and $(NH_4)_2CO_3$ (separately) to bright redness on platinum foil. Treat any residue that may remain in each case with dilute HCl. Give reasons for the phenomena observed.

23. Place a little finely divided $CaCO_3$ in a flask ; pour in about 100 cc. of water charged with CO_2, cork the flask and let stand for some hours, with occasional shaking. Filter. Boil the filtrate for fifteen minutes, keeping the volume constant by the addition of distilled water.

Explain the observed results. How do they bear upon the question of " boiler scale ? "

24. Take 1,000 cc. of water *"temporarily hard,"* and *"soften"* it by " Clark's process."—(*Watts' Dict.*, 5, 1026 ; also *Wanklyn's Water Analysis*, 118.)

25. Shake up some powdered marble with a little water, and see if the liquid give any reaction on test paper. Heat another portion of marble to intense redness in a platinum crucible, cool, and shake that up also with a little water. Test this liquid also with test paper. Explain the course of the different results obtained.

26. Ignite a very small fragment of marble on charcoal before the blowpipe, and notice the white "glow" pro-

duced.   What use is made of this property in the arts?—
(*Wagner's Chem. Technology,* 664.)

Did the ignition cause any change in the marble?

27. Place about fifteen grammes of "quicklime" in twenty-
five cc. water. Stir with a thermometer and note the change
in temperature. Has chemical reaction taken place? Will
evolution of heat always follow chemical reaction?—(*Rich-
ter's Chem.,* 65.)

28. Place some clear lime-water in a beaker and leave it
exposed to the atmosphere for an hour or two. Note and
explain the result. What bearing has this upon the "har-
dening" of mortar?—(*Payen's Industrial Chem.,* 285.)

29. By the aid of a pneumatic trough fill a test-tube with
H_2S. With the open end of the tube still under water, slip
in a small lump of lime and close the end firmly with the
thumb.   Shake the tube and notice the suction on the
thumb. While under water, remove the thumb slightly
and note the rise of water in the tube. What has taken
place, and how does it bear upon the purification of coal
gas?—(*Payen's Industrial Chem.,* 705.)

30. Mix a little "plaster of Paris" with its own bulk of
water, pour into a paper mold and allow it to "set."
When hard, place the casting in the water oven until per-
fectly dry. Introduce some of this dry mass into a glass
tube closed at one end and heat in Bunsen flame. Is water
given off? Was it hygroscopic moisture only? What is the
chemistry of the "setting" of "plaster of Paris?"—
(*Payen's Industrial Chem.,* 287.)

31. Place five grammes "bleaching powder" in a tall beaker.
Pour over it ten cc. dilute H_2SO_4. Notice the odor of the
gas evolved. Take a piece of litmus paper three inches
long, dip half of it in water and hold the paper in the fumes
evolved from the "bleaching powder." Notice the difference between the action upon the moist as compared with
the dry portion of the paper. Why this difference? What
is "bleaching powder"? What action have acids upon it?
(*Payen's Indus. Chem.,* 169; *Roscoe & Schorlemmer,* 1, 120.)

Barium.—Use solution of $BaCl_2$.

32. H_2SO_4: heavy, white, finely divided precipitate of $BaSO_4$—insoluble in all ordinary reagents.

(Where acids are required as reagents, always use *dilute* unless *concentrated* be specified.)

33. $(NH_4)_2CO_3$: white precipitate of $BaCO_3$, soluble in acetic acid.

34. K_2CrO_4: yellow precipitate of $BaCrO_4$, insoluble in acetic acid. (Different from Ca and Sr.)

35. *Flame coloration*—Yellowish green.
(Examine by the spectroscope.)

36. Compare the specific gravity of " heavy spar" (use the Jolly balance) with that of "marble." Is " weight"a characteristic of the compounds of barium?

37. To 500 cc. "permanently hard" water add a few cc. $BaCl_2$ solution. Would water so treated, and afterward filtered, form " boiler scale?" Give reasons.—(*Watts' Dict.*, 1, 715.)

Strontium.—Use $Sr(NO_3)_2$.

38. H_2SO_4: white precipitate of $SrSO_4$. Slowly formed in cold solutions, but immediately on boiling.

39. $(NH_4)_2CO_3$: white precipitate of $SrCO_3$, soluble in acetic acid.

40. K_2CrO_4: yellow precipitate of $SrCrO_4$, soluble in acetic acid. (Different from Ba and Ca.)

41. *Flame Coloration*—Crimson.

(Examine by the spectroscope.)

Iron.—(FERRIC SALTS.)   Use Fe_2Cl_6.

42. K_4FeCy_6:   Dark-blue   precipitate — " Prussian blue."—$Fe_4(FeCy_6)_3$.

43. $K_6(FeCy_6)_2$: no precipitate.   (Different from ferrous salts.)

44. KCyS : blood-red coloration—$Fe(CyS)_3$.

45. $(NH_4)_2S$: black precipitate of FeS, mixed with white sulphur.

46. NH_4OH : reddish flocculent precipitate of Fe_2 $(OH)_6$; soluble in acids; insoluble in KOH.   The presence of sundry organic substances (*e. g.*, sugar, tartaric acid) will prevent this precipitation.   Try this.

47. H_2S : sulphur separates and the ferric is reduced to ferrous chloride. $Fe_2Cl_6 + H_2S = 2FeCl_2 + 2HCl + S$.

48. Borax bead : $\begin{cases} \text{Oxidizing flame....yellow.} \\ \text{Reducing flame....green.} \end{cases}$

To make the bead test, plunge the red-hot loop of platinum wire into powdered borax and then hold it in the Bunsen flame until the adhering borax is fused to a *colorless*, transparent glass.   If the substance under examination be a powder, place a *very little* thereof upon the bead, fuse thoroughly before the blow-pipe, and examine when cold.   If the substance be liquid, dip the bead into the same and reheat many times, or, preferably, evaporate a portion of the liquid and examine the residue as a solid.)

Iron.—(FERROUS SALTS.)   Use $FeSO_4$.

49. K_4FeCy_6 : light-blue precipitate—$FeK_2(FeCy_6)$.

50. $K_6(FeCy_6)_2$: dark-blue precipitate—" Turnbull's blue"—$Fe_3(FeCy_6)_2$. (Different from *ferric* salts.)

51. KCyS : no reaction. (Different from *ferric* salts.)

52. NH_4OH : green precipitate of $Fe(OH)_2$, turning reddish where exposed to the air. The presence of sundry organic substances (*e. g.*, sugar, tartaric acid) will prevent this precipitation. Try this.

53. In each of two beakers place some cast iron filings. Add dilute HCl and warm until no further action takes place. A dark residue remains. What is it? Add to one of the solutions a few cc. strong HNO_3 and heat to nearly boiling. Cool. Make each solution alkaline with NH_4OH and note the different appearance of the precipitates. Give equations for all that has taken place.—(*Fresenius Qual.*, 141 and 143.)

54. To a few cc. of an aqueous solution of gallic acid, add a drop of Fe_2Cl_6 solution. Note the change. Now add a few crystals of oxalic acid, shake, and again note the change. How does this bear upon the preparation of common ink, and the removal of ink stains from fabrics?—(*Watts' Dict.*, 3, 270.)

Chromium.—Use $KCr(SO_4)_2$.

55. NH_4OH : green precipitate of $Cr_2(OH)_6$, soluble in acids. The presence of sundry organic substances (*e. g.*, sugar, tartaric acid) will prevent this precipitation.

Is this precipitate soluble in strong NH_4OH? Try it.

56. KOH : green precipitate of $Cr_2(OH)_6$, soluble in an excess of the precipitant, from which solution it is again deposited on boiling, or on addition of NH_4Cl.

57. $(NH_4)_2S$: same precipitate as above, the reaction being: $2KCr(SO_4)_2 + 3(NH_4)_2S + 6H_2O = Cr_2(OH)_6 + K_2SO_4 + 3(NH_4)_2SO_4 + 3H_2S$.

58. If any chromium compound be fused on platinum foil with a mixture of Na_2CO_3 and $NaNO_3$, yellow Na_2CrO_4 will be formed. If this yellow mass be dissolved in water, the solution acidulated with acetic acid, and boiled, a yellow precipitate of lead chromate, $PbCrO_4$, will appear immediately upon the addition of lead acetate, $Pb(C_2H_3O_2)_2$.

This test is highly characteristic.

Upon addition of the acetic acid, why does an effervescence take place?

59. Pass H_2S or H_2SO_3 into a solution of potassium chromate and note the change in color accompanying the reduction of the chromate to a salt of chromium. Repeat the experiment, using potassium dichromate.

60. Borax bead—green.

Aluminum.—Use $K_2Al_2(SO_4)_4$.

61. NH_4OH: white flocculent precipitate of $Al_2(OH)_6$, best seen on boiling. Soluble in acids and in KOH. The presence of sundry organic substances (*e. g.*, sugar, tartaric acid) will prevent this precipitation. Try this.

62. KOH: white precipitate of $Al_2(OH)_6$, soluble in excess of precipitant, from which solution it may again be thrown down by acidifying with HCl, adding NH_4OH to alkaline reaction, and boiling.

63. $(NH_4)_2S$: white precipitate of $Al_2(OH)_6$. Reaction similar to paragraph 59.

64. To a solution of alum add a little solution of Na_2CO_3. Is the precipitate a carbonate? Try this after filtering the precipitate off and washing it. Carbonates effervesce with acids.—(*Watts' Dict.*, 1, 159 and 779).

65. Fill a beaker with water and add a little solution of Brazil wood until the water is slightly tinted pink. Add a few cc. solution of alum and then make slightly alkaline with ammonia. After standing a few moments, shake and filter. What is the nature of the precipitate? Is the coloring matter still in solution? How does this bear upon the question of dyeing?—(*Watts' Dict.*, 2, 352).

66. To a liter of "peaty" water add about 0.02 gramme alum dissolved in a little water; mix and let stand over night. Note the result. Does the water taste of alum? Is the above the amount of alum that in average cases gives good results?—(*Chem. News*, 51, 242.)

Zinc.—Use $ZnSO_4$.

67. $(NH_4)_2S$: white precipitate of ZnS, soluble in mineral acids, insoluble in acetic acid.

68. H_2S: same as above.

(In solutions acidulated with mineral acids, no precipitate is formed, and even in neutral solutions the precipitation is but partial, owing to the acid formed during the reaction.)

69. KOH : white precipitate of $Zn(OH)_2$, soluble in excess. (Different from Mn.)

70. K_4FeCy_6: white precipitate of Zn_2FeCy_6.

71. Zinc compounds (solid), when heated before the blowpipe, on charcoal, in the reducing flame, de-

posit a non-volatile coating of ZnO upon the charcoal. This coating is yellow while hot and white when cold. If the coating be moistened with a drop of $Co(NO_3)$, solution and be again ignited, it will become *yellowish-green* in color.   (Compare paragraph 138.)

For a list of the coatings on charcoal, see page 55.

Manganese.—Use $MnSO_4$.

72. $(NH_4)_2S$: light-pink precipitate of MnS, soluble in acids.

73. H_2S : no precipitate in presence of acetic acid, owing to MnS being soluble therein. (Different from Zn.)

74. KOH : white precipitate of $Mn(OH)_2$, which turns brown on exposure to air from the formation of $Mn_2(OH)_6$.

Insoluble in excess of KOH.   (Different from Zn.)

75. Borax bead : $\begin{cases} \text{Oxidizing flame..amethyst.} \\ \text{Reducing flame..colorless.} \end{cases}$

76. Any manganese compound fused on platinum foil with Na_2CO_3, and $NaNO_3$, will form a *bluish-green mass*, Na_2MnO_4, which will impart its own color to the solution if it be dissolved in water.   HCl destroys the color of such solution.   (Compare paragraph 58.)

77. Note by experiment that the green color of solutions of manganates and the purple color of permanganates are entirely removed by the addition of reducing agents, such as H_2S or H_2SO_3, which cause a reduction to colorless salts of manganese.

78. Nearly fill two glass-stoppered bottles with distilled water made acid with H_2SO_4. To *one* of them add a few drops of a weak solution of sugar or other organic material. To *each* of them add the same number of drops of a solution of potassium permanganate. The contents of each bottle should now be a bright pink. Set them aside for several hours and then note the difference in their appearance.

Has this any bearing upon the examination of potable waters ?—(*Watts' Dict.*, 5, 1029.)

It would be well to repeat the above using distilled water in one bottle and ordinary tap water in the other with no addition of sugar to either.

Cobalt.—Use $Co(NO_3)_2$.

79. $(NH_4)_2S$: black precipitate of CoS, insoluble in dilute HCl. If a crystal of $KClO_3$ be dropped into the tube and the liquid boiled, the CoS will be rapidly decomposed.

(HCl and $KClO_3$ react on each other with the production of Cl and ClO_2, a most powerful oxidizing mixture:

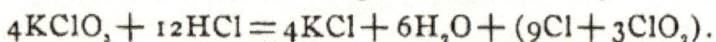

$$4KClO_3 + 12HCl = 4KCl + 6H_2O + (9Cl + 3ClO_2).$$

This mixture is termed " Euchlor," and wherever, in these notes, the expression is employed, $KClO_3$, HCl and heat are indicated.)

80. KCy : reddish precipitate of $CoCy_2$; soluble in excess; re-precipitated by HCl.

81. KOH : blue precipitate of $Co(OH)_2$. Very strong solution of KOH dissolves this precipitate to a blue liquid upon application of heat.

82. Borax bead : deep blue.

83. A dilute solution of cobalt chloride may be used as a

sympathetic ink. Writing executed with it remains colorless until heated, when it turns blue. Try it. Explain this action.—(*Payen's Industrial Chem.*, 514.)

Nickel.—Use $Ni(NO_3)_2$.

84. $(NH_4)_2S$: black precipitate of NiS, insoluble in cold dilute HCl. Decomposed by "Euchlor." Partially soluble in an excess of the precipitant; show this by adding much $(NH_4)_2S$, heating and filtering. The filtrate will be of a dark color, due to the dissolved NiS. Boil this solution until it ceases to smell of $(NH_4)_2S$, keeping the volume constant by the addition of water; the NiS will be again precipitated.

85. KCy : greenish precipitate of $NiCy_2$, soluble in excess; reprecipitated by HCl.

86. Slightly acidulate a solution of nickel with a few drops of HCl; add a weak solution of KCy until the precipitate of $NiCy_2$ at first formed is redissolved; boil this solution for some minutes, keeping the volume constant by addition of water; add KOH to strong alkaline reaction; heat nearly to boiling and then add large excess of bromine water; a black precipitate of $Ni(OH)_3$ will appear.

87. Borax bead : $\begin{cases} \text{Oxidizing flame}\cdots\text{reddish brown.} \\ \text{Reducing flame}\cdots\text{smoky.} \end{cases}$

Mercury.—(MERCURIC SALTS.)   Use $HgCl_2$.

88. H_2S : precipitate of HgS, at first white, then yel-

low, and finally black ; soluble in "aqua regia ;" insoluble in $(NH_4)_2S$, or in any single acid.

(" The white precipitate which forms at first, consists of a double compound of mercuric sulphide with the still undecomposed portion of the mercuric salt."—*Fresenius*.)

89. $SnCl_2$: white precipitate of Hg_2Cl_2.

$$2HgCl_2 + SnCl_2 = Hg_2Cl_2 + SnCl_4.$$

The test is more delicate if the solutions be warmed.

If the $SnCl_2$ be added in large excess, the precipitate will be black from the presence of separated mercury :

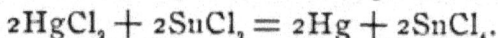

$$2HgCl_2 + 2SnCl_2 = 2Hg + 2SnCl_4.$$

90. Any compound of mercury (mercuric or mercurous) in the dry state, if mixed with two or three times its bulk of dry Na_2CO_3, and heated in a glass tube, closed at one end, will yield small globules of metallic mercury as a sublimate upon the cooler portions of the tube. (Where the metal is not readily seen at once, the sublimate should be carefully raked with a wooden tooth-pick in order to cause the microscopic particles to coalesce to a visible size. Always hold the tube in the fingers, otherwise it may become too hot to condense the mercury.)

91. NH_4OH : white precipitate of NH_2HgCl. (Different from mercurous.)

92. KI : red precipitate of Hg_2I. (Different from mercurous.)

93. HCl : no precipitate. (Different from mercurous).

94. Dip a clean copper coin into $HgCl_2$ solution slightly acidified with HCl. A white amalgam will at once form upon the coin.

Mercury.—(Mercurous Salts. Use $Hg_2(NO_3)_2$.

95. H_2S: black precipitate of Hg_2S.

96. NH_4OH: black precipitate of $NH_2Hg_2NO_3$. (Different from mercuric.)

97. KI: green precipitate of Hg_2I_2. (Different from mercuric.)

98. HCl: white precipitate of Hg_2Cl_2. (Different from mercuric.)

99. "Corrosive sublimate," $HgCl_2$, and "calomel," Hg_2Cl_2, are two very common salts of mercury. The following points should be noted for their distinction: 1. General appearance. 2. One of them is soluble in hot water. Which one? 3. How do they differ when heated in a glass tube closed at one end? 4. Pour some NH_4OH upon each and note results.

100. Is $HgCl_2$ poisonous? Is it an effective disinfectant?— (*Chem. Applied to the Arts.*, 3, 615.)

Lead.—Use $Pb(C_2H_3O_2)_2$.

101. H_2S or $(NH_4)_2S$: black precipitate of PbS. (This precipitate will be at first red if much HCl be present.) Insoluble in $(NH_4)_2S$. Soluble in hot, dilute HNO_3. Oxidized to $PbSO_4$ by boiling with concentrated HNO_3.

102. HCl: white precipitate of $PbCl_2$, soluble in hot water.

103. H_2SO_4: white precipitate of $PbSO_4$; may be dissolved by pouring upon it acetic acid, then adding ammonium hydroxide in excess and boiling.

104. Na_2CO_3: white precipitate of $PbCO_3$.

105. K_2CrO_4: yellow precipitate of $PbCrO_4$; very insoluble in acetic acid.

106. On charcoal before the blowpipe, reducing flame, lead salts give a *yellow* coating, surrounded by more or less white.

107. Place some lead shavings in a flask containing distilled water. Let stand for a day with occasional shaking. Decant the water from the lead and pass H_2S. How does the observed result bear upon the question of city water supply?—(*Watts' Dict.*, 3, 478.)

108. Rub up some " white lead " and some " zinc white," separately, with a little water. Smear some of each on any flat surface, and determine which material would furnish the better paint for use in an atmosphere contaminated with H_2S.

Copper.—Use $CuSO_4$.

109. H_2S or $(NH_4)_2S$: black precipitate of CuS; soluble in HNO_3; also in KCN; insoluble in $(NH_4)_2S$.

110. KOH: blue precipitate of $Cu(OH)_2$. Changes to black CuO on boiling.

111. NH_4OH: blue precipitate, which dissolves in an excess of the reagent to a deep blue solution of $(N_2H_6Cu)SO_4$. Color destroyed by KCN.

112. K_4FeCy_6: chocolate-colored precipitate of Cu_2FeCy_6; insoluble in acetic acid.

113. Na_2CO_3: greenish-blue basic salt, $CuCO_3.Cu(OH)_2$ changes to black on boiling.

114. Acidulate a copper solution with a few drops of H_2SO_4, and dip into it a bright, clean knife blade; the

latter will become coated with metallic copper. Also place in the above solution a platinum foil upon which is laid a fragment of zinc ; metallic copper will deposit upon the platinum.

115. Borax bead: $\begin{cases} \text{Oxidizing flame..light blue.} \\ \text{Reducing flame..red and opaque.} \end{cases}$

116. *Flame reaction*—usually green.   (See page 54.)

Bismuth.—Use $Bi(NO_3)_3$, dissolved in dilute HCl.

117. H_2S : black precipitate of Bi_2S_3 ; soluble in HNO_3 ; insoluble in $(NH_4)_2S$.

118. H_2O : when added in large quantity, a white precipitate of BiOCl.

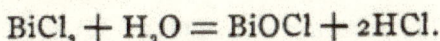

$$BiCl_3 + H_2O = BiOCl + 2HCl.$$

(This precipitate is readily soluble in mineral acids, but is insoluble in $H_2(C_4H_4O_6)$, by which it may be distinguished from SbOCl. See paragraph 130. It is changed to black Bi_2S_3 upon passing H_2S.)

119. $(NH_4)OH$: white precipitate of $Bi(OH)_3$, soluble in acids.

120. Heated alone before the blowpipe, reducing flame, bismuth compounds give a *yellow* coating on the charcoal similar to lead ; but if heated in the reducing flame with a mixture of equal parts of potassium iodide and sulphur, a brilliant *crimson* coating will be formed.

Cadmium.—Use $CdCl_2$.

121. H_2S or $(NH_4)_2S$: yellow precipitate of CdS ; soluble in hot HNO_3 ; insoluble in KCN.

122. Na_2CO_3 : white precipitate of $CdCO_3$; the precipitation is prevented by free ammonia.

123. Before the blowpipe, reducing flame, on charcoal a *brown* coating is formed which is often *iridescent*.

Silver.—Use $AgNO_3$.

124. H_2S : black precipitate of Ag_2S ; insoluble in $(NH_4)_2S$; soluble in HNO_3.

125. HCl : white precipitate of $AgCl$; turns purple on exposure to sunlight ; soluble in NH_4OH, from which solution it is again precipitated by HNO_3.

Arsenic.—Use solution of As_2O_3 in HCl.

126. H_2S : yellow precipitate of As_2S_3 ; soluble in both $(NH_4)_2S$ and $(NH_4)_2CO_3$, from which solutions it is again precipitated by acidifying with HCl.

127. If any compound of arsenic in the dry state be mixed with powdered Na_2CO_3 and KCN, and the mixture heated in a small glass tube closed at one end, metallic arsenic will be deposited on the cooler portions of the tube. If the closed end of the tube be now cut off and the sublimate heated, white As_2O_3 will form, and on further heating will volatilize with a characteristic *garlic odor*.

128. If mixed with a little Na_2CO_3 and KCN and heated on charcoal in the reducing flame, arsenic compounds give a garlic odor and produce a volatile, *white* coating on the charcoal.

Antimony.—Use $SbCl_3$.

129. H_2S : orange precipitate of Sb_2S_3 ; insoluble in $(NH_4)_2CO_3$; soluble in $(NH_4)_2S$, from which solution it is reprecipitated by HCl.

130. H_2O: white precipitate of SbOCl ; soluble in mineral acids, and also in $H_2(C_4H_4O_6)$. Different from BiOCl. (See paragraph 118.) The white precipitate of SbOCl will change to orange Sb_2S_3 upon passing H_2S. Under similar circumstances the white BiOCl would change to black Bi_2S_3.

131. Metallic zinc placed upon platinum foil and immersed in an acid solution of $SbCl_3$, will cause a black deposit of metallic antimony to appear upon the platinum. This stain is soluble in hot dilute HNO_3. Dilute and cool the HNO_3 solution thus obtained and pass H_2S. An orange precipitate of Sb_2S_3 will appear.

132. If mixed with a little Na_2CO_3 and KCN, and heated on charcoal in the reducing flame, antimony compounds give a volatile *white* coating. Touched with a drop of $(NH_4)_2S$ this coating will assume an orange color. (See also page 55.)

Tin. (STANNOUS SALTS.)—Use $SnCl_2$.

133. H_2S : brown precipitate of SnS ; soluble in *yellow* $(NH_4)_2S$, from which solution it is thrown out by the addition of HCl as yellow SnS_2.

134. $HgCl_2$: white precipitate of Hg_2Cl_2. (See paragraph 89.)

Tin. (STANNIC SALTS.)—Use $SnCl_4$.

135. H_2S: yellow precipitate of SnS_2; soluble in $(NH_4)_2S$; reprecipitated by HCl.

136. $HgCl_2$: no reaction. (Different from stannous salts.)

137. Metallic zinc, added to any solution of tin, stannic or stannous, acidulated with HCl, will cause a deposit of metallic tin to take place. Action is hastened by placing platinum foil under the zinc, and applying gentle heat. The deposit may be recognized by removing the undissolved zinc (after removing any adhering particles of deposit), pouring off the liquid, heating the residue with a little strong HCl and pouring into it a hot solution of $HgCl_2$. A white precipitate indicates tin. (See paragraph 89.)

138. On charcoal, in the reducing flame, tin compounds give a non-volatile *white* coating. If moistened with cobalt nitrate solution and again ignited, this coating will turn *bluish-green*. (Compare zinc, paragraph 71.)

Reactions for the Acid Residues.

Sulphates.—Use $(NH_4)_2SO_4$.

139. $BaCl_2$: white precipitate of $BaSO_4$, insoluble in any reagent.

140. When testing an unknown substance for the presence of a sulphate, it is necessary to acidify the solution with HCl and boil before adding the $BaCl_2$ solution. Show this by adding $BaCl_2$ to a solution of Na_2CO_3 both with and without the previous addition of HCl as above directed.

141. If Ag, Pb or Hg' be present in the solution, $Ba(NO_3)_2$ must be used instead of $BaCl_2$, otherwise chlorides of the the above metals would be precipitated. In this case HNO_3 must be used for acidifying the solution in place of HCl.

142. Add $BaCl_2$ to concentrated HCl; a white precipitate of $BaCl_2$ separates out. Note its crystalline structure, and the fact of its being readily soluble in water after decanting the acid, facts that do not hold good for the precipitate obtained from presence of a sulphate. To avoid this precipitation, when testing for a sulphate, always see that the solution is dilute before adding the barium reagent.

143. If any solid sulphur compound be mixed with twice its bulk of Na_2CO_3, and the mixture be thoroughly fused upon charcoal in the reducing flame, the fused mass removed, crushed, placed upon a silver coin, and moistened with a drop or two of water, a black stain of Ag_2S will appear upon the coin.

144. *Free sulphuric acid* may be detected by mixing a *very little* white sugar with a portion of the solution and evaporating to complete dryness over a water-bath; the

residue will be black from the charring action of the H_2SO_4.

Paper dipped into the solution and dried in the same manner will become blackened.

(Blue litmus paper will be reddened by free sulphuric acid, but that is a reaction common to all acids.)

145. Are normal sulphates usually soluble in water? What are the exceptions?

146. Does sulphur exist in coal? To determine this fuse some powdered coal with $NaNO_3$ and Na_2CO_3 in a porcelain crucible; dissolve in water; acidify with HCl; boil; filter if necessary, and test the filtrate for a "sulphate." In what condition does sulphur exist in coal?—*J. Chem. Soc.*, 38, 708.

Carbonates.—Use Na_2CO_3.

147. Any of the mineral acids will cause an effervescence of CO_2, which gas is to be recognized as follows: half fill a test-tube with *fresh* lime-water, generate the CO_2 in another tube and decant the gas (only) into the former; a white pellicle of $CaCO_3$, forming upon the surface of the lime-water, constitutes the test.

Why should the lime-water be fresh?

148. *Free carbonic acid* never exists unless in aqueous solution, and is decomposed by heat into water and carbonic oxide. Therefore simply boil the solution and conduct the steam, by means of a bent glass tube, into fresh lime-water. A white precipitate of $CaCO_3$ shows presence of H_2CO_3. [$(NH_4)_2CO_3$ would all pass over, with the steam if present in the solution.]

149. By aid of a piece of glass tubing blow through some clear lime-water for a few moments. Note and explain the result.

150. Place a *little* organic matter of any kind in a glass tube open at both ends. Connect one end with an aspirator and arrange a flask of lime-water so that the air drawn through the tube will bubble through the lime-water. At the other end of the tube, also place a flask of lime-water (or KOH), so as to free the air from CO_2 before it enters the tube. Start the aspirator and place a lamp under the organic matter in the tube. Note the resulting milkiness of the lime-water. Was the carbon in the organic substance present as a "carbonate?"

Sulphides.—Use FeS.

151. The mineral acids cause an effervescence of H_2S; recognized by its smell and by its blackening paper moistened with $Pb(C_2H_3O_2)_2$.

152. Solutions of soluble sulphides [use $(NH_4)_2S$] give a black stain when dropped upon silver coin, and also give a black precipitate of PbS when treated with $Pb(C_2H_3O_2)_2$.

153. *Free hydrosulphuric acid*, H_2S : recognized by its smell, and by its blackening paper moistened with $Pb(C_2H_3O_2)_2$.

154. Acidify some yellow ammonium sulphide solution (See page 52) with HCl. What is the precipitate formed?— *Fresenius Qual.*, 237.)

155. Will all strong acids decompose H_2S? Try several.

156. What are the products of the combustion of H_2S? Prove this. (See sulphites.)

Sulphites.—Use Na_2SO_3.

157. If HCl be added and the solution warmed, SO_2

will be given off, which may be recognized by its smell (that of burning sulphur), and by its turning a solution of $K_2Cr_2O_7$ green. (Dip a glass rod into a solution of $K_2Cr_2O_7$, and hold it in the atmosphere of SO_2, the adhering drops of $K_2Cr_2O_7$ will be turned green.)

158. *Free sulphurous acid*, H_2SO_3; best recognized by its smell of SO_2, and by its turning $K_2Cr_2O_7$ green.

Nitrates.—Use $NaNO_3$.

159. To a solution of a nitrate in a test-tube, add an equal bulk of strong H_2SO_4; mix and *cool thoroughly*. Incline the tube as nearly horizontal as possible, and gently pour into it a cold strong solution of $FeSO_4$. The latter solution will float upon the heavy acid mixture, and at their line of separation a dark ring will form, highly characteristic of a nitrate.

(Where the nitrate solution is very dilute, this ring will often not appear until after several minutes.)

160. *Free nitric acid*, HNO_3, gives the dark color with $FeSO_4$ alone, without the aid of H_2SO_4. It is better to drop a few crystals of $FeSO_4$ into a test-tube containing the liquid to be tested, rather than use a solution, as in 159. The dark color appears near the crystals.

161. { Why is H_2SO_4 used in 159?
What general statement may be made as to the solubility of nitrates.

162. Boil five grammes gunpowder in fifty cc. water, filter, and prove presence of KNO_3 in the filtrate. Warm the residue with some special solvent for sulphur (*Storer's Dict. Solubilities*); filter, evaporate the solution to dryness on the water-bath and ignite the residue, noting the smell and

action on $K_2Cr_2O_7$ (see paragraph 157). Prove that the black material left after filtering off the sulphur solution contains carbon (see paragraph 150).

163. If heated before the blowpipe on charcoal, would a nitrate oxidize the carbon? Try it.

Chlorates.—Use $KClO_3$.

164. Add indigo solution until a very faint blue color is produced, keeping the liquid *cool;* then add a little Na_2SO_3 or H_2SO_3, and shake. The blue color is destroyed.

165. Under what circumstances would the presence of a nitrate interfere with this test? Determine this by experiment.

166. Strong H_2SO_4, added to a chlorate in the solid state, liberates a readily explosive oxide of chlorine, if the mixture be warmed.

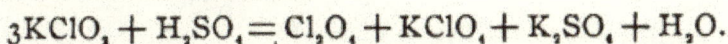

$$3KClO_3 + H_2SO_4 = Cl_2O_4 + KClO_4 + K_2SO_4 + H_2O.$$

(Use but a small quantity and keep the test-tube pointed away from the face.)

167. Place some $KClO_3$ in a glass tube closed at one end. Apply heat from a Bunsen burner and hold a glowing match stick in the open end of the tube; what is indicated? Does a similar decomposition take place with all chlorates, or is it peculiar to $KClO_3$ alone?—(*Watts' Dict.*, 1, 885.)

168. Heat a chlorate to redness in a porcelain crucible; when cool dissolve the mass in hot water, and add $AgNO_3$. A white precipitate of AgCl shows the presence of a chloride, which same came from the decomposition of the original chlorate.

169. What general statement may be made with reference to the solubility of chlorates as a class?

Chlorides.—Use NH_4Cl.

170. $AgNO_3$ gives a white precipitate of AgCl, readily soluble in cold NH_4OH, from which solution it is again precipitated by acidifying with HNO_3. (Exposed to sunlight, this precipitate rapidly turns violet.)

171. Dissolve some copper oxide in a bead of salt of phosphorus by use of the oxidizing flame. While still hot, touch the bead to any substance containing chlorine so as to cause some of the same to adhere to the bead. Upon reheating in the oxidizing flame a fine blue flame will appear.

172. *Free hydrochloric acid* liberates chlorine when heated with pure MnO_2. The chlorine may be recognized by its bleaching action on moistened blue litmus paper.

Cyanides.—Use KCN.

173. $AgNO_3$: white precipitate of AgCN; easily soluble in NH_4OH.

174. Make a solution of a cyanide alkaline with NH_4OH; then add $(NH_4)_2S$ in slight excess. Filter off any precipitate that may form. Heat the filtrate until all $(NH_4)_2S$ has been given off, keeping the volume constant by addition of water. Now acidify with HCl and add a drop or two of Fe_2Cl_6; a blood-red coloration constitutes the test.

175. *Detection of chlorides in presence of cyanides:* Precipitate both as silver salts by addition of $AgNO_3$ solution. Filter and ignite the precipitate in a *porcelain*

crucible.   The cyanide of silver will be decomposed.
Fuse the residue with Na_2CO_3 and $NaNO_3$, extract with
water, acidulate with HNO_3, boil and add $AgNO_3$ solution.   A white precipitate indicates the presence of a
chloride.   (See paragraph 170.)
(Write all the equations involved in this process.)

Bromides.—Use KBr.

176. $AgNO_3$ gives a yellowish-white precipitate of
AgBr, soluble with great difficulty in cold NH_4OH, but
more easily soluble if the solution be heated. HNO_3 re-
precipitates it from this solution.

177. Add a few drops of chlorine water and shake.
Bromine is liberated.

$$KBr + Cl = KCl + Br.$$

If a few drops of CS_2 be now added and the liquid
shaken, the bromine will become dissolved in the CS_2,
and will color it reddish-brown.

(An excess of chlorine-water must be avoided, otherwise colorless $BrCl_3$ would be formed.)

(Chloroform may be employed in place of CS_2.)

Iodides.—Use KI.

178. $AgNO_3$ gives a yellow precipitate of AgI, insoluble in NH_4OH.

179. To a solution of an iodide add an excess of cold
starch solution (made by boiling one part of starch in
one hundred parts of water, and cooling), then a few

drops of chlorine water ; a blue precipitate of iodide of starch immediately appears.

180. If the precipitate obtained in 178 be heated with strong H_2SO_4, vapors of iodine will be evolved. If in too small quantity to be readily seen, hold a glass rod, previously moistened with starch solution, in the atmosphere of the test-tube ; blue iodide of starch will appear up the rod.

181. If an iodide solution be treated as in 177, the CS_2 will be turned violet. (In this case also, avoid an excess of the chlorine water.)

182. *Detection of chlorides, bromides and iodides when mixed :* Heat the solution under examination and add a solution of Cu_2SO_4 prepared by mixing $CuSO_4$ with either $FeSO_4$ or H_2SO_3 ; *iodine*, if present, will be precipitated as Cu_2I_2. Filter. Discard the precipitate and test filtrate for complete precipitation.

Make filtrate alkaline with KOH, and evaporate to dryness.

Mix the dry residue with about twice its bulk of dry $K_2Cr_2O_7$. Introduce the mixture into a dry flask ; mix it with concentrated H_2SO_4, warm, and conduct the evolved gas, by means of glass tubing, into water contained in another test-tube. When action ceases, divide the water through which the gas has been passed, into two parts ; in one portion test for *bromine* with CS_2, as in paragraph 177 ; to the other add NH_4OH in excess, then acetic acid to acid reaction, and finally a few drops of $Pb(C_2H_3O_2)_2$; a yellow precipitate indicates presence of *chlorine*.

Phosphates.—Use Na_2HPO_4.

183. In dilute solutions, NH_4HMoO_4 (dissolved in nitric acid), gives a yellow granular precipitate, which readily appears upon shaking. The precipitate is easily soluble in alkalies.

(Arsenates also give a yellow precipitate with this reagent, but only upon boiling.)

184. Add NH_4Cl; make alkaline with NH_4OH, and then add $MgSO_4$; a white precipitate of $MgNH_4PO_4$ will appear. Precipitate readily soluble in acids. (This test is of value only in the absence of arsenates.)

185. Thoroughly dry a substance containing a phosphate. Place the pulverized material, together with a small piece of magnesium wire, in a mattrass, and heat intensely before the blowpipe. Cool; break the mattrass and moisten the mass with *one drop* of water. The characteristic odor of hydrogen phosphide will be evolved.

Borates.—Use $Na_2B_4O_7$.

186. Place a solid borate in an evaporating dish, moisten it with strong H_2SO_4, add a little alcohol and set fire to the mixture; the flame will be colored green upon its edges.

187. Mix a borate with a little strong HCl, dilute a little, dip a piece of turmeric paper into the mixture and dry it by holding it over a small flame (being careful to avoid charring); the paper will appear brown, and if moistened with NH_4OH, will become nearly black.

188. *Free boric acid* (H_3BO_3) is a white solid, soluble in water. It may be recognized by its turning blue litmus paper red and by giving the tests described in paragraphs 186 and 187, *without* the aid of H_2SO_4 and HCl.

189. What action has the strong H_2SO_4 in paragraph 186 and the HCl in paragraph 187.

Fluorides.—Use CaF_2.

190. Coat the convex side of a watch-glass with beeswax, and trace a design upon the wax. Place some powdered CaF_2 in a porcelain crucible; moisten it thoroughly with strong H_2SO_4; cover the crucible with the prepared watch-glass and set it aside for an hour or more. The design will be found etched upon the surface of the glass.

If but little fluoride be present, the design may best be seen after breathing upon the cold surface of the glass.

Ferro-Cyanides.—Use K_4FeCy_6.

191. Fe_2Cl_6: precipitate of "Prussian blue," $Fe_4(FeCy_6)_3$.

192. $CuSO_4$: Chocolate-colored precipitate. $Cu_2(FeCy_6)$.

193. $FeSO_4$: light-blue precipitate. $FeK_2(FeCy_6)$.

Ferri-Cyanides.—Use $K_6(FeCy_6)_2$.

194. $FeSO_4$: dark-blue precipitate of $Fe_3(FeCy_6)_2$.

Sulpho-Cyanides.—Use KCyS.

195. Fe_2Cl_6 : blood-red coloration. $Fe(CyS)_3$.

Silicates.

196. If a silicate in solution be acidified with HCl and evaporated to dryness on the water-bath, all the silica present will separate as white SiO_2, and may be filtered off from aqueous solution of the dry mass.

(It is better after evaporating to dryness to moisten the dry mass with strong HCl, let stand a few moments, and then add hot water, stir and filter.)

197. Take half a gramme of some insoluble silicate (*e.g.*, clay), pulverize finely, fuse in a platinum crucible with four times its bulk, of a mixture of equal parts of K_2CO_3 and Na_2CO_3, cool. Boil with water, filter from any undissolved residue, and show that silica is present in the filtrate.

Scheme for Complete Analysis.

BASIC RESIDUES.

(The substance is supposed to be liquid. If solid, refer to page 47.)

Set aside one-half, to be tested for the acid residues (see page 50) and which may also serve as a reserve in case of accident.

(*a*) Take the flame reaction. (Paragraph 9 and page 54.)

(*b*) Examine with the spectroscope.

(*c*) Make the borax-bead test. (Paragraph 48.)

(*d*) Test for ammonium salts by heating with KOH. (Paragraph 2.)

(*e*) Note the color and smell, and take the reaction on test paper. If the reaction be *alkaline* refer to page 51.

After short preliminary examinations, proceed at once to the General Table.

GENERAL TABLE.

Add dilute HCl until no further precipitate is formed, heat gently, filter and wash once with *cold* water.

Precipitate: —Chlorides of Ag, Hg', Pb. Examine by Table I.

Filtrate: —If not already dilute, add water to make it so (disregarding any precipitate that may form), pass H_2S until the liquid after thorough stirring, smells strong of the reagent, warm, filter and wash.

    Precipitate: —Sulphides of Pb, Hg'', Cu, Bi, Cd. Also of As, Sb, Sn. Examine by Table II.

    Filtrate: —Boil until smell of H_2S is gone. Add a little strong HNO_3, and evaporate to dryness. (If organic matter be present ignite the dry residue.) Moisten thoroughly with strong HCl, add hot water and heat. Filter off any separated *silica*. Add NH_4OH to alkaline reaction, boil, filter.

        Precipitate: —Hydrates of Fe, Cr, Al. Examine by Table IV.

        Filtrate: —Add $(NH_4)_2S$ in slight excess, heat, filter and wash.

            Precipitate: —Sulphides of Co, Ni, Mn, Zn. Examine by Table V.

            Filtrate: —Boil until it ceases to smell of $(NH_4)_2S$, keeping the volume constant by addition of water. If any sulphide of nickel separate (par. 84), filter it off, and to the now clear filtrate add $(NH_4)_2 CO_3$ warm, filter and wash.

                Precipitate: — Carbonates of Ba, Sr, Ca. Examine by Table VI.

                Filtrate: —This final filtrate is to be examined for Mg and K, by Table VII.

| Silver Group. | Copper and arsenic Groups. | Iron Group. | Zinc Group. | Barium Group. | Potassium Group. |

The reagents here successively employed are termed "group reagents," and are to be memorized as such. The given order of testing must be strictly follo*v*ed, for it is a rule, to which there are unimportant exceptions, that any group reagent will precipitate not only its own group, but also those which precede it. One will thus readily see the importance of separating *all* of a group before adding to the filtrate the reagent for the group below. In every case, therefore, test the filtrate for any further precipitation before adding the next reagent.

In every case where a precipitate is obtained, it must be thoroughly washed (unless otherwise directed) with hot water, either by decantation or else directly upon the filter. Were this washing omitted, much of the filtrate would remain in the pores of the precipitate, and the analysis of the latter might be seriously interfered with.

Use enough of a group reagent to do the work of completely precipitating its group, but do not add a large quantity beyond what is necessary, inasmuch as such a great excess will often interfere with the separating of the groups below.

Strong barium solutions are precipitated by HCl (see paragraph 142), but such precipitates, being readily soluble in cold water, are easily distinguished from those of the silver group.

If a yellowish solution turn green upon passing H_2S, chromium, originally present as a chromate, is indicated. Again, if a green or purple solution become colorless, the presence of manganese, originally present as a manganate, or permanganate, is shown. A separation of sulphur will usually be observed to accompany these changes. (See paragraphs 59 and 77.)

Organic matter must be removed before adding the reagent for the iron group for the reasons given in paragraphs 46, 52, 55, and 61.

HCl having been added before the iron group reagent (*i. e.*, NH_4OH) causes NH_4Cl to be formed. The presence of this latter salt is necessary to prevent hydrates of other metals (especially Zn and Mg) being thrown down with those of the iron group. Metallic hydrates below the iron group are soluble in NH_4Cl.

TABLE I.   SILVER GROUP.—Ag, Hg', Pb.

———

Treat the precipitate produced by HCl with boiling water.
Filter and wash.

Filtrate :—Acidify with acetic acid. Add a few drops of K_2CrO_4.	*Precipitate :*—Treat what remains upon the filter paper with warm NH_4OH. Filter.	
	Filtrate :—Acidify with HNO_3.	*Precipitate :*—The fact of the residue having been *turned black* by the NH_4OH is alone an indication of a mercurous salt (par. 96). Confirm by drying the precipitate and heating it with Na_2CO_3 in a glass tube closed at one end (par. 90). Minute globules of metallic mercury indicate presence of
A yellow precipitate indicates presence of LEAD.	White precipitate indicates presence of SILVER.	MERCUROSUM.

TABLE II. COPPER GROUP.—Pb, Hg'', Cu, Bi, Cd.

Place the precipitate produced by H_2S in a beaker; cover it with yellow $(NH_4)_2S$; warm and stir for some minutes. Filter. The filtrate will contain the *arsenic group,* which examine by Table III. After washing the residue, place it in an evaporating dish, cover it with strong HNO_3, and evaporate on water-bath *nearly* to dryness. Dilute with water, add a little H_2SO_4; stir, filter, and wash.

Precipitate:—That remaining on the filter paper may consist of HgS, mixed with $PbSO_4$. Remove it from the filter paper; cover it with acetic acid; add NH_4OH in excess; boil and filter.		*Filtrate:*—Add NH_4OH to alkaline reaction; boil and filter.	
Precipitate:—Dry, mix with dry Na_2CO_3 and heat in a glass tube, closed at one end (paragraph 90).	*Filtrate:*—Acidify with acetic acid. Add a few drops of K_2CrO_4.	*Precipitate:*—Dissolve in a little hot HCl and pour this solution into a large quantity of cold water.	*Filtrate:*—If blue in color, copper is indicated. Divide into two portions:
Globules of metallic mercury indicate presence of MERCURIC.	Yellow precipitate indicates presence of LEAD.	White precipitate indicates presence of BISMUTH.	*First portion.*—Acidify with acetic acid. Add a few drops of potassium ferrocyanide. A chocolate colored precipitate indicates presence of COPPER. / *Second portion.*—Add KCN solution until blue color disappears, then add a little $(NH_4)_2S$. A yellow precipitate indicates presence of CADMIUM.

TABLE III.   ARSENIC GROUP.—As, Sb, Sn.

To the solution of the group in $(NH_4)_2S$ (see beginning of Table II), add HCl to *faintly acid* reaction : the dissolved sulphides will be reprecipitated.[1] Filter and reject the filtrate. Cover the precipitate with $(NH_4)_2CO_3$—stir for about half a minute and filter.

Filtrate : —Add dilute HCl to *just acid* r e a c t i o n. Boil. A yellow precipitate of As_2S_3 indicates presence of ARSENIC.	*Residue :*—Dissolve in a little hot concentrated HCl. Dilute with water. Place a piece of metallic zinc, supported on platinum foil, in the solution ; let them remain about a minute. A black stain on the platinum constitutes the test for antimony. To confirm this, place the foil in a dish ; drop upon it *one or two drops* of concentrated HNO_3 ; add $H_2(C_4H_4O_6)$ and water, and boil ; the precipitate dissolves. To the solution add H_2S ; an orange-colored precipitate of Sb_2S_3 shows presence of ANTIMONY. Remove the platinum, but let the zinc remain in solution. Add more zinc, if necessary. As soon as hydrogen ceases to be evolved, remove the remaining zinc, rinsing off into the dish any adhering material. Let the deposit settle ; decant the liquid ; wash once by decantation ; dissolve a little hot HCl ; filter (after slight dilution) if necessary, and pour into a hot solution of $HgCl_2$. A white precipitate indicates TIN.

[1] The sulphides of the arsenic group are all yellow, orange or brown ; a white or dirty gray precipitate, obtained upon acidifying with HCl, indicates a separation of sulphur only. (Paragraph 154.)

TABLE IV. IRON GROUP.—Fe, Cr, Al.

Cover the precipitate, obtained on adding NH_4OH, with a solution of KOH; boil and stir for some minutes; filter.

| *Filtrate:*—Acidify with HCl, then make alkaline with NH_4OH, and boil.

A colorless, gelatinous precipitate indicates presence of

ALUMINUM.[1] | *Residue :* — Consists of $Fe_2(OH)_6$ and $Cr_2(OH)_6$. Place it upon a platinum foil with upturned edges (paper and all if necessary), and dry by holding high above the Bunsen flame. When dry add two or three times its bulk of dry Na_2CO_3, a little $NaNO_3$, and fuse. If the fused mass be *yellow* when cold, *chromium* is indicated. As this color may be at times obscured,[2] place the foil in a small dish and boil with water until the mass is all dissolved except dark brown Fe_2O_3. Filter. | |
| | *Filtrate :*—Acidify with acetic acid, boil for several minutes, and add a few drops of $Pb(C_2H_3O_2)_2$. A yellow precipitate indicates presence of

CHROMIUM. | *Residue :* — Dissolve in a little hot concentrated HCl. Add water and then a few drops of $K_4Fe(CN)_6$. A blue precipitate indicates presence of

IRON. |

[1] A slight precipitate will usually appear, even in the absence of aluminum, because of the impurity commonly present in the KOH.

[2] When manganese is present it will often be precipitated in the iron group, and will then exhibit its characteristic *bluish-green* mass when treated with fusion mixture on platinum foil.

TABLE V. ZINC GROUP.—Co, Ni, Mn, Zu.

Place the precipitate produced by $(NH_4)_2S$ in a beaker, cover it with *cold, very dilute* (about 1 to 20) HCl, and stir for a moment. Filter and wash.

Precipitate :—(Test with borax bead.) Dissolve in "Euchlor" (paragraph 79), and divide into two portions.		*Filtrate :*—Boil until smell of H_2S is gone. Add a few crystals of $KClO_3$, and again boil until all sulphur is oxidized. Cool. Make strongly alkaline with KOH. Stir, filter, and wash.	
First portion :—Evaporate nearly to dryness; dilute; add KCN solution until the precipitate at first formed is just redissolved. Boil for some minutes; add KOH in excess; heat nearly to boiling and add a large excess of bromine water. A black precipitate indicates	*Second portion:*—Make alkaline with KOH and filter. Without washing, place some of the precipitate in a test-tube, add a piece of solid KOH and a *very* little water (only enough to dissolve the KOH). Boil for a few minutes and set the tube aside for a short time. Any solid matter present will shortly settle and if the *solution* above it be *blue* the indication is	*Precipitate :* — Fuse with Na_2CO_3 and $NaNO_3$ on platinum foil	*Filtrate:*—Acidify with HCl. Make alkaline with NH_4OH and add K_4FeCy_6. A white precipitate indicates
		Bluish green mass indicates	
NICKEL.	COBALT.	MANGANESE.	*ZINC.

* Confirm this by testing before the blowpipe on charcoal (paragraph 71).

TABLE VI. BARIUM GROUP.—Ba, Sr, Ca.

The precipitate produced by $(NH_4)_2CO_3$ is first examined by the spectroscope and flame reactions. Afterwards dissolve the precipitate in a little hot acetic acid. Dilute. Add K_2CrO_4 in excess, warm and filter.

Precipitate:—Of a yellow color indicates presence of	*Filtrate:*—Add NH_4OH to alkaline reaction; then $(NH_4)_2CO_3$ in excess. Filter. Reject the filtrate. Dissolve the precipitate in a little hot acetic acid. Dilute considerably. Add dilute H_2SO_4 in slight excess. Boil and filter.	
	Precipitate:—(White) indicates presence of	*Filtrate:*— Add NH_4OH to alkaline reaction and then a solution of ammonium oxalate.
		A white precipitate indicates presence of
BARIUM.	STRONTIUM.	CALCIUM.

TABLE VII.   POTASSIUM GROUP.—Mg, K, Na, NH_4.

Traces of the barium group are liable to still exist in this final filtrate, and should be removed therefrom by adding to the hot liquid a few drops of $(NH_4)_2SO_4$ solution, and also a little solution of ammonium oxalate. Flter off and discard any precipitate that may form. Cool. To the now clear filtrate add a solution of Na_2HPO_4. Filter.

Precipitate: — (White) indicates presence of	Filtrate :—(To be examined for K only, as Na and NH_4, if present, will have been already detected in the preliminary examination.)
	Evaporate to dryness. Place residue on platinum foil, and heat at low redness until fumes cease. Test portion of what remains by spectroscope for K.
	Heat the remainder (foil and all) in a *very little* water, to which a drop or two of HCl has been added. When solution is complete, pour upon watch-glass, add few drops of $PtCl_4$ and a little alcohol and stir. A yellow precipitate indicates presence of
MAGNESIUM	POTASSIUM.

ANALYSIS OF SOLIDS.

(A) METALS AND ALLOYS.

See if the metal be magnetic (cobalt, nickel and iron are magnetic). Try its fusibility before the blowpipe and its coating on charcoal (page 55). Heat a little in a mattrass and observe if mercury be given off. Finely divide the metal, if possible. Place it in a flask and heat with rather dilute HCl (equal parts water and acid). If complete solution take place, examine at once by General Table. If not, add more HCl and a little strong HNO$_3$, and reheat until all metal has disappeared and only a white residue remains.[1] Dilute slightly and filter :

Filtrate :— Still further dilute and then (disregarding any precipitate that diluting may cause), examine at once by General Table, omitting the silver group.	*Residue :*—Boil with water and filter :	
	Filtrate :—Acidify with acetic acid and add K$_2$CrO$_4$. Yellow precipitate indicates	*Residue :*—Soluble in warm NH$_4$OH, from which it is again precipitated by addition of HNO$_3$ indicates
	LEAD.	SILVER.

(B) NON-METALLIC SOLIDS.

Moisten a little of the substance with strong HCl and take the flame and spectroscope reactions. Place a small portion upon moistened test paper and observe its reaction.

Determine the reaction on charcoal before the blowpipe. (Page 55.) Try the "silver coin" test for sulphur. (Paragraph 143).

[1] A black residue of carbon will at times be noticed, as when cast iron is being acted upon. This may be proved to be carbon by paragraph 150.

Make the remaining preliminary tests given on page 36.

Ignite a portion on platinum foil. If charring take place, organic matter is present.

By the aid of a microscope some little insight as to the nature of the organic matter may at times be obtained.

The smell of *burning feathers* during ignition indicates the presence of organic matter containing *nitrogen*.

If the organic matter be of an oily or fatty nature it may be removed by solution in ether or petroleum naphtha.

Heat different small portions of the substance with :

(*a*) Water.

(*b*) Hydrochloric acid dilute.

(*c*) Hydrochloric acid concentrated.[1]

(*d*) Aqua regia.

If complete solution be effected by one of the above solvents,[2] treat a larger portion of the substance to be analyzed with the same.   Evaporate the greater portion of the acid, if one have been used ; dilute largely and examine by General Table.

If only a portion dissolve, filter, examine the filtrate by the General Table and treat the residue as an insoluble substance.   (See page 49.)

(Always examine the water solution for K, Na and NH,, as salts of those metals are soluble in that liquid.)

[1] It is well to bear in mind that salts of silver and lead that may have been insoluble before, will be converted by this treatment into $PbCl_2$ (which is soluble in hot water) and AgCl (which is soluble in warm NH_4OH). The residue after heating with HCl should therefore be treated with hot water, filtered and tested for *lead*, and afterwards treated with warm NH_4OH, filtered, and tested for *silver*, before going further in the analysis.

[2] If the water solution (*a*) should have an *alkaline* reaction refer to page 51.

INSOLUBLE SUBSTANCES.

Mix the finely divided substance with about three parts of " fusion mixture" (equal parts of K_2CO_3 and Na_2CO_3) add a *very* little $NaNO_3$ and fuse in a platinum crucible.

When cool, place crucible and contents in a beaker, cover with water, and heat until the mass be disintegrated. Filter and wash. Remove a small portion of the filtrate and test for a *chloride*.

To the rest of the filtrate, by itself, and to the undissolved mass, by itself, add concentrated HCl to strong acid reaction, and evaporate to complete dryness on the water bath.

Moisten each dry mass with strong HCl, add water and heat until everything except *white SiO_2* has gone into solution. Filter, and examine each filtrate by General Table.[1]

(Do not forget to report the SiO_2 when found).

[1] Place a little of one of the filtrates in a test-tube and add a little of the other. If no precipitate be produced, the bulks of the two filtrates may be mixed and analyzed as one liquid, otherwise they must be kept separate.

EXAMINATION FOR ACID RESIDUES.

Test separate portions of the original substance for the several acids according to the directions given in paragraphs 139 to 197, the presence of one acid not interfering with the detection of others.

Notes.—Always acidify with HCl and boil before adding $BaCl_2$, in testing for a sulphate.

Likewise acidify with HNO_3 and boil before testing with $AgNO_3$ for any of the Halogens.

If the precipitate produced by $AgNO_3$ be yellowish, indicating the presence of I or Br, or both, it will be best to remove all the bases of the upper groups before attempting the separation of these two halogens. Therefore boil with an excess of Na_2CO_3, filter, reject the precipitate, neutralize with HNO_3, boil until all CO_2 be removed, make slightly alkaline with KOH, and proceed as per paragraph 182.

Solids soluble in HCl may be tested for a chloride by fusing with " fusion mixture," dissolving fusion in hot dilute HNO_3, boiling, filtering if necessary, and adding $AgNO_3$ to filtrate.

ANALYSIS OF LIQUIDS ORIGINALLY ALKALINE.

Acidify a small portion with HNO_3. If no precipitate fall, or only separation of white sulphur occur, proceed as usual. Should a precipitate fall, acidify the whole liquid strongly with HNO_3; evaporate to dryness on the water bath; add dilute HNO_3, heat and filter. Make the filtrate alkaline with NH_4OH, and then add HCl to acid reaction : If a precipitate should fall, filter and add it to that already obtained. Examine filtrate by General Table.

Boil residue with water, filter and test filtrate for *lead*.

After extracting the lead, warm the residue left on the filter paper with NH_4OH, filter and test filtrate for *silver*. The final residue will be *silica*.

APPENDIX.

PREPARATION OF REAGENTS.

NH_4HMoO_4.—Dissolve one part of molybdic acid in four parts of ammonia, and pour the solution into fifteen parts of dilute nitric acid of sp. gr. 1.20 (equal parts nitric acid and water). Let stand a day or two and filter.

FeS.—Heat small nails to redness in a large graphite crucible, throw in roll sulphur until the mass be fused, pour out and cool.

H_2S.—One part common H_2SO_4 is diluted with twelve parts water, cooled and poured into the apparatus containing the FeS.

$(NH_4)_2S$.—Dilute strong ammonia with its own volume of water, and then pass a slow current of H_2S until the solution will turn paper moistened with lead acetate to a dark color.

  "Yellow" ammonium sulphide $(NH_4)_2S_n$ is prepared by dissolving a little powdered sulphur in the reagent prepared as above.

TEST PAPERS (*from Fresenius*).

  Blue Litmus.—Digest one part litmus of commerce with six parts water, filter, divide filtrate into equal parts, saturate the free alkali in *one* part by repeatedly stirring with a glass rod previously dipped in very dilute H_2SO_4, until the color just appears red. Pour the two portions together again, draw strips of unsized paper through the solution, and hang them up to dry.

Reddened Litmus Paper.—Stir the above blue litmus solution with a glass rod previously dipped in dilute H_2SO_4, until the solution appear red, and then draw strips of paper through, as above.

Turmeric Paper.—Digest one part bruised turmeric root with four parts alcohol and two of water, filter, draw strips of paper through the solution, and dry as before.

THE DILUTE ACIDS AND DILUTE AMMONIUM HYDROXIDE, as ordinarily used, are prepared by adding the following amounts of water (by volume) to the concentrated articles :

> 1 part HCl to 4 parts water.
> 1 part H_2SO_4 to 4 parts water.
> 1 part HNO_3 to 5 parts water.
> 1 part NH_4OH to 3 parts water.

THE FOLLOWING SALTS may be bought in the solid form and made into solution by dissolving one part by weight of the salt in the following amounts of water :

> $(NH_4)_2CO_3$,...... 8 parts water and 1 part NH_4OH.
> NH_4Cl .... 10 parts water.
> $(NH_4)_2C_2O_4$ ..... 24 parts water.
> KOH .... 10 parts water.
> K_2CrO_4 .... 10 parts water.

Na_2HPO_4 ······· 10 parts water.
$K_4Fe(CN)_6$ ······ 12 parts water.
Na_2CO_3 ········· 10 parts water.
$BaCl_2$ ··········· 10 parts water.
$MgSO_4$ ·········· 8 parts water.
$Pb(C_2H_3O_2)_2$ ···· 10 parts water.
$HgCl_2$ ··········· 20 parts water.
$AgNO_3$ ·········· 20 parts water.
$Co(NO_3)_2$ ······· 10 parts water.

COLORED FLAMES.

YELLOW··············Sodium compounds.
RED ···············Calcium compounds.
CRIMSON ···········Strontium compounds.
VIOLET ············Potassium compounds.
BLUE ··············Copper chloride, lead, arsenic, antimony.
GREEN·············Hydrochloric acid, boric acid, phosphoric acid, barium salts, copper compounds, except the chloride.
GREENISH-WHITE···Zinc.

BORAX BEADS.

	Reducing flame.	Oxidizing flame.
Iron	green	yellow.
Chromium	green	green.
Manganese	colorless	amethyst.
Cobalt	blue	blue.
Nickel	smoky	brown.
Copper	opaque red	light blue.

EXAMINATION ON CHARCOAL.

Before the blowpipe, reducing flame, either alone or mixed with Na_2CO_3, the compounds of some metals give characteristic coatings on the charcoal:

ANTIMONY: *White and volatile.* If the coating be scraped off, placed upon platinum foil, and a drop of HCl and a granule of zinc added, a *black stain* will appear upon the foil. (See also paragraph 132).

ARSENIC: *White and volatile.* Gives *garlic* odor.

BISMUTH: *Yellow.* If the substance be mixed with a mixture of equal parts of KI and S and ignited in the reducing flame the coating will appear *crimson.*

CADMIUM: *Brown* and often iridescent.

LEAD: *Yellow.*

SILVER: *Red-brown.*

TIN: *Yellow* when *hot,* *white* when *cold.* If the coating be moistened with $Co(NO_3)_2$ solution and again ignited, it will turn *bluish-green.*

Zinc: Same as tin, except that the coating turns *yellow-ish-green* if treated with $Co(NO_3)_2$ solution.

Note.—Chlorides of the metals being more or less volatile, false "chloride coatings" will often appear upon the charcoal if the assay be heated without flux. Such a coating for lead, for instance, would be white in place of the true oxide color. The student should memorize the colors of the common metallic oxides.

CARE OF PLATINUM VESSELS.

1°. Always use either platinum or pipe clay support.

2°. With exception of manganese, avoid fusing salts of members of the silver, copper, arsenic and zinc groups.

3°. Avoid "aqua-regia," "euchlor," or free chlorine.

4°. Avoid sulphides of metals.

5°. Avoid alkaline nitrates (in quantity), hydrates or cyanides.

6°. Always clean crucibles *thoroughly;* remove stains by gentle friction with sand or powdered fluor-spar. Never use force to detach any lump adhering from previous fusion, but extract same with water and HCl, or else by fusion with a little $KHSO_4$ and subsequent washing.

www.ingramcontent.com/pod-product-compliance
Lightning Source LLC
Chambersburg PA
CBHW022037080426
42733CB00007B/861